Explore Your Unconscious Mind

7 practices to find balance, serenity, and energy for your everyday life

By Thanos Kyng

Until you make the unconscious conscious, it will direct your life and you will call it fate.
—Carl Gustav Jung

We Dedicate this Book to all the great Masters of the Past and to all the great Apprentices of the Present. May the Future be for Us a Temple to the Virtues built on the cornerstone of Consciousness.
∴ Ordo Ab Chao ∴

"EXPLORE YOUR UNCONSCIOUS MIND: 7 practices to find balance, serenity and energy for your everyday life"

by Thanos Kyng

Published by Mind Training International LTD

© 2019 London

Thanos Kyng
Visit my website www.thanoskyng.com

Isbn: 9781077455481

DISCLAIMER

Although the author and publisher have made every effort to ensure that the information in this book was correct at press time, the author and publisher do not assume and hereby disclaim any liability to any party for any loss, damage, or disruption caused by errors or omissions, whether such errors or omissions result from negligence, accident, or any other cause.

Nothing on this book is intended to diagnose, treat, or cure any medical condition of whatever nature, and shall not be construed as medical advice, implied or otherwise.

The contents of this book are intended to be for informational, educational and for edification purposes only. Always seek the advice of your doctor with any questions you may have regarding a medical condition.

Index

Preface

Once upon a time, in a very distant place lived a wise and powerful King. In the land he controlled and administered, lived, and prospered many individuals, animals and, some say, creatures that now no longer exist.

King of his land where he lived and worked, he also had the opportunity to travel and meet people from other distant lands.

Every day he was carrying on with his busy life, growing up, caring for his loved ones, supporting his kingdom, and performing his duties effectively.

As in all realms, he must face every day unexpected events, economic turmoil, discontent, external attacks, but also beautiful things like successes, promotions, gifts, new births, friendships, and new relationships.

The King at some point realized that it was time to seek more from his earthly experience, from his daily life, as he understood that he could do much more than he already did and learn much more than he already had.

At some point the King had heard about a famous Mage; a person that was able to communicate with the deepest part that is in each one of us. This individual appeared often in his kingdom and so the King decided to get in touch with him and to call him in order to discuss the deepest questions that were in his mind and for which he was seeking answers.

And so, the Mage, got invited by the King and after a couple of days he arrived at court.

The King commanded everyone else to leave the throne hall so that he could be alone with the Mage and ask him all the questions and most private and profound things which were on his mind.

And so, the King began to ask multiple questions whilst expecting a clear and resolutive answer from this mystical individual that the Mage was.

After each question of the King a profound silence reigned in the room...

The King was beginning to grow impatient as he started to think that this person, the Mage, could be a charlatan or an imposter, as he was not responding to any of the questions and stood there in silence.

At some point the Mage began to respond; making some unexpected questions to the King, as if he was trying to make him understand even better what the profound nature of those questions was.

Seated on his throne he was amazed by the nature of the questions and began to think deeper; he started remembering things, feeling sensations, seeing images that never, before that exact moment, had been able to successfully remember and recall...

∞ ∞ ∞

And here we are in this book that will accompany you through the 7 Keys, 7 simple practices to reach, obtain, and maintain a serene and a conscious state of mind whilst starting to Explore Your Unconscious Mind.

Why did I choose these seven practices?

The reason is quite simple. Having and maintaining a mental state of serenity and calmness is a simple skill that requires only continuous practice and determination.

After years of studying in applied Neuroscience and Hypnotherapy I have come to identify these simple practices, that you will soon see and put into practice yourself, as some of the most effective.

The method is straightforward and consists in focusing your attention and your full awareness in the present moment, in the here and now.

By doing so, you will be able to accept and express calmly, in a healthy manner and without judgement all your thoughts, emotions and sensations.

Which are the benefits of these practices in your daily life?
Let us have a look at some important benefits:

- You will be able to mitigate and even get rid of symptoms such as anxiety, stress, and fear.

- You will be able to focus more on yourself and learn how to avoid thinking too much about your past or fearing of a potential future that has not happened yet.
- You will be in tune with your physical body, and you will be able to perceive yourself even better.
- You will start to pay attention on your breathing patterns. In many traditions the breath is considered as the spirit and the soul and as you will see, when you will focus on your breathing, you will create space and time for yourself and your perception and awareness will increase; giving you access to your higher self and spirituality itself.
- You will be kinder, and more delicate towards yourself because you will know and understand how to accept your thoughts and emotions while avoiding judging yourself on a rational and logical level.
- You will find it easier to balance your emotional, mental, and physical state.
- You will learn how to allow your mind to rest, because remember that even when the brain rests during sleep, the mind never does so.

The fundamental thing to understand before moving forwards in this book is to fully understand how strong your intention and your will is.

Know that a weak determination will take you not far from where you are now, even if you have the most effective of practices and the most incredible knowledge available to you.

It is incredibly important that you deal with these 7 Keys with the same intention, commitment, and determination that you apply to things, activities, and relationships in which you have the most success in your life!

Awake the pure child that is still in you and embrace this new experience with enthusiasm, happiness, and a sensation of a profound Wonder!

You have nothing to lose and everything to get!

The 7 keys

Before we start using our 7 Keys to open some of the doors of the unconscious mind and to get the best out of these practices, here are some guidelines for your practice to become more efficient.

1. Take a comfortable position. It is not necessary to be in a special or difficult position because the important thing is for you to have a relaxing and a pleasant experience.
   The more you become familiar and practical, the more you can have fun studying and learning whilst in different positions and techniques to advance through practicing.
   For now, sit comfortably on the bed, on the couch, or where you feel the most comfortable.

2. Be kind to yourself and start with small steps. As in during a meditation and in any other practices it is important to train your mind to relax and to access the quietness of it.
   The less we are accustomed to do it the more our mind will tend to deflate and drift away from the quietness you are looking to access.
   Learn to create an initial practice and whenever you feel to take a break, even if it is just for a few seconds or minutes, just do it, and then start again.
   A Teacher of mine once said to me: "It's hard to know how to design a perfect circle. But if you start by designing

small dots along the surface, at some point you will be able to create the circle with simplicity and ease ".

Same thing applies during the practice; is it possible to stay in the quietness of the mind for 30 minutes? Yes of course. You need to be consistent and persistent to achieve anything you invest yourself into.

3. It is not a competition. We are not here to ask for obstacles or objectives to be avoided or achieved. You started reading this book so that you can enjoy the freedom of your mind, to create a space of your own without limits and conditions. A space and a time in which to be in contact with your true and profound higher self.

4. Create a habit and repeat it as many times during a week as you can, preferably at the same time, on a specific day, so that your unconscious mind will be able to register this new activity and accept this practice as a new habit. And by doing so it will help you to make your experience even more pleasant and effective each time you will repeat it.

Key #1

Focus Exercise

●

With this Key #1 you will practice and experience concentration and then you will start to train your mind to bring all your attention, and focus, on a particular moment of the present. The here and now.

This is a quite simple practice that will immerse you towards the increasingly effective use of your ability to focus.

Also, you can apply this practice in any other situation and area of your life in which you feel the need, to be present, to improve your focus and to be in the here and now.

You will be able to improve your performance in all areas of your life and enjoy much more the process rather than just the result.

The most intense and beautiful part of the path you choose, and journey of your life, is the process; more so than achieving the outcome.

Good Practice!

Focus Exercise

- Sit or lie down in a comfortable and relaxing position, in location or space where you feel and are safe.

- Choose an item that you can easily hold in both hands. It can be anything you like as long as it feels comfortable to you. For example, a fruit.

- While you are holding it with both hands in front of you, start by putting your full attention on this item of your choice.

- Direct your energy and thoughts towards what you have placed in your hands, right now.

- Use your senses to thoroughly explore this object that you are holding and direct your attention to every little detail that you can perceive and sense.

- Look at all the colors, textures, pigments, surface, and composition.

- Perceive every little sound that comes from moving the object in your hands, or if it is a fruit you have chosen try chewing it.

- Explore, touch, and pay attention to every little signal of sensation generated by the contact between your skin and the object.

- Pay attention to every sensation and emotion that is present in your body right now.

- Use your olfactory sense to smell the object and perceive the different layers of smell and fragrance coming from it.

- Put your attention in every flavor, and taste, that you can discern right now.

- And now, start again from the first point and repeat the process until you feel you are in a moment of tranquility, serenity and be surprised by how many things you have managed to notice more than ever before, in such a simple and pleasant way.

When the conscious mind and the Unconscious are in conflict, the Unconscious Mind always wins, without exception.

– *Simon Knight*

Key #2

Explore your Body Exercise

The practice of Key #2 will accompany you through a sweet and pleasant exploration of every part of your body. It is a wonderful exercise to do, to reconnect with your temple (your body) physically, emotionally, and spiritually.

This very easy to do practice is probably the most powerful and effective one in order to consolidate a healthy connection, through breathing, between your mind and body.

Thanks to this exercise you will explore and experience the present moment, the Now, and you will reconnect to the deepest parts of yourself, since you will have the pleasure of listening and perceiving all your being without paying attention to the outside world.

The practice of this Key is a magnificent gift you are making to yourself.

Explore your Body

- Take the most comfortable position possible, in a safe space. For this exercise I recommend lying down on a bed or a couch.

- Do not use pillows to lift your head; keep your head and every part of your body at the same level, and imagine as if you were lying on a soft and smooth lawn, on a beautiful day, with a perfect and pleasant temperature, in which you feel completely relaxed, now.

- The practice begins by closing your eyes, and start inhaling and exhaling more intensely and deeper than your usual breathing; for three (3) consecutive times, slowly.

- Relax the muscles of your face, of your eyelids, all the muscles around your eyes, above the eyebrows, as well as every little muscle on your cheeks; relax the muscles of your mouth and eventually every muscle until you reach the neck and as follows, bring this feeling and awareness of relaxation to the rest of your body, all the way down to your feet.

- Now pay your utmost attention to your breath, to the air that enters and exits through your nostrils, and blends into the air of this beautiful day, which happily reaches also down in to your lungs, and expands more and more this moment of relaxation while you are sitting or lying on this lawn.

- Now, starting from your forehead, your third eye, focus your attention on this part of your body, breathe through your forehead and perceive every fragment of skin, every cell and every little detail you can see and perceive from that specific point in which, right now, you put all your attention to.

- After the forehead move your attention to all the other parts of your body, starting from the head and reaching down to the rest of your body until you reach the soles of your feet.

- This practice allows you to pay attention to every single part of your body and you will be able to discover and perceive new information and details of your physical body that before this very moment were, probably for you, unknown or taken for granted.

- Repeat this practice as often as possible and if it is difficult to explore the whole body in a single session you can decide and choose precisely which parts of the body you can focus and work on for each single practice.

It is a characteristic of an evolved mind to entertain a thought even without accepting it.

- Aristotle

Key # 3

Awareness Exercise

O n Key #3 you exercise on how to obtain total awareness in a practical and efficient way within your daily activities.

This practice is amazing because it allows you to put more attention on your daily actions that otherwise you would have taken for granted and that on many occasions run on complete automatism, without granting yourself the gift of being present in whatever it is that you are doing.

It is a practice suitable for any moment of the day and it is very effective because, unlike other practices, it does not require you to sit or lie down; therefore you can experience it on every occasion that fits you, inspires you the most and motivates you!

Exercise of Awareness

Think of one or more actions that you undertake during your daily life and think about how many times everything happens in an automatic manner. It may be the streets you are driving on to go to work or it could be the routine you have to brush your teeth before you go to sleep.

Here are some examples of situations where you can use this exercise and you will be able to understand how it works and how it easily fits in any situation you want.

- While using your toothbrush, focus your attention on the action you are doing: feel the touch between your toothbrush and your hand, the muscles of your arm contracting, the sensation of your teeth, the taste of toothpaste, every sound you can hear and perceive during the action and notice everything you see, and if you are looking in the mirror observe every little detail of your face, of the toothbrush and everything else you are seeing right now.

- As you wash the dishes, feel the temperature of the water, the density of the dishes, the glasses, hear the sound of the sponge when it is rubbed against a dish and the scent of the detergent you are using. Look at every color and every nuance, pay attention to every sound around you and every movement you are making right now.

- As you are on your way to work, pay attention to every little detail you encounter on the road: People's faces, their expressions, imagine what they might be thinking while walking or moving, see the details of the environment and nature around you, of the trees, of the sky, and while you do this, keep your attention on the route you are undertaking. And while you are present and notice all the above, today, change course. Take a different street than your usual so that you can put even more attention on everything you encounter or do and on the whole new route itself.

- While writing something, while cooking or while reading a book and even while using your smartphone, try and change the hand which you would normally use. If you use the right hand now use the left hand instead and vice versa. This change helps you to keep your attention level high and stay in the present moment, in the now. In addition, in doing so you can access other parts and paths of your brain both motorial and mnemonic.

The *mind is not a vessel to be filled but a fire to be kindled.*

– *Plutarch*

Key #4

Gratitude Exercise

The practice of Key #4 consists of elements that can change your life in an incredible way.

Often getting carried away from a hectic lifestyle, full of thoughts; most of the times negative or dysfunctional ones, we forget to realize and celebrate what we already have in our lives, instead of keeping on chasing what we want or what we think we want; or what we do not have or possess.

Every so often we need to have a moment of peace with ourselves, to sit or lie down, and realize how fortunate we are to have everything we already have and that everything has been given to us by life and by our decisions and actions.

This is an exercise that helps you be in the present moment, in the now. It helps you to appreciate, even more, all that is around you in your life, be it objects, people, animals, or other...

This practice is one of those milestones that has forever changed for the better the lives of the greatest leaders, and of the greatest minds in our history.

To be able, in fact, to understand the value of what there is around us and understand how fortunate we are, is an extremely powerful automatic connection with the present moment, the Now, which brings us to the point to live our lives with more joy, gratitude, happiness and love.

In addition, this practice helps you prepare yourself to embrace all the abundance you will receive and gain in your future.

Exercise of Gratitude

- Take a comfortable position where you can relax, in a safe space as in previous practices.

- Breathe deep with your eyes closed and begin to relax your mind, bringing your attention to your breath.

- Feel every sensation of your body and everything you feel coming from the room or space where you are right now. Pay attention to your breath and everything you see in your mind while you are present, in the here and now.

- Open your eyes and think of all the things that, now, you feel grateful for having in your life. It can be anything, probably even something that until now you took absolutely for granted and which is important to be thankful for, for example: The gift of speech, your legs, a healthy mind, loved ones, the house in which you live in, the job you have, etc....

- Think of all the above as a precious gift to you and for you because there is definitely someone who is hoping, imagining, praying or struggling to even have a small piece of what you own, and which you have at the moment.

- Use a personal notebook or diary and the pen you like the most. (e.g. color, shape, texture)

- Write down at least 3 (three) things that you are thankful for and the reason **Why**!

- Repeat this practice as many times as possible weekly/daily even without writing and you will see soon enough that your unconscious mind will recognize this exercise as a habit of yours, as part of your daily routine and it will come easier to you to be thankful for what life gives you or brings your way.

To make this practice even more effective, I suggest you find a stone or a crystal of your preference that you can easily hold with both of your hands.

Repeat the above exercise and squeeze the stone or crystal with the both of your hands and concentrate in order to pour into the stone or crystal all these wonderful thoughts, sounds, feelings, and images of yours.

After the exercise, put the stone or crystal on your bedside table or anyplace next to the bed or space you sleep in.

When you wake up in the morning and before you go to bed the fact of seeing the stone or the crystal will automatically bring your mind to the present moment and remind you of all the gratitude you have filled your life with so far!

The shaping of your character is happening
through your choices, day by day.
What are your interests?
What are your thoughts?
What are your deeds?
This you will become.

– Heracletus

Key #5

Explore the Nature Exercise

$\mathcal{K}$ ey #5 would seem like a foregone or forsaken practice, but how to get in touch with nature and how to perceive every single detail is an incredible practice that will help you reconnect with yourself and fully live in the present moment.

There are many ways to accomplish the above and it is not really necessary to have time or have access in forests and grasslands; the important thing is to be able to grant yourself a moment of peace where you can be on your own, undisturbed, in the midst of nature or the environment you find yourself in.

When I speak of nature, I mean multiple situations, environments, or places and now I will list some examples for you, of how to enjoy this practice and this exercise to the maximum.

Explore Nature

- Walk barefoot on grass and while you do so, pay attention to every sensation that comes from the contact of your feet with the grass and Mother Earth. At some point sit or lie down while maintaining contact between your feet and the turf. Close your eyes, breathe deeply and imagine as if from the soles of your feet emerge roots made of light, of a color and shape that you like the most, and that immerse themselves in the earth beneath you. With every breath, you feel the energy of Mother Earth communicating with every inch of your being and every part of you, as you now see, feel, and perceive everything around you and within you.

- In a forest, a meadow or wherever there are trees and you can be serene, choose a tree that you like the most and place your back on its trunk by leaning on it. You are barefoot and imagine the same scene as the above example whilst this time you perceive your back in contact with the trunk of the tree as you immerse yourself in this beautiful experience. As the tree perceives feelings by being immersed inside the earth imagine how many things it knows, have seen and experienced of the world while being there, standing strong, where you find yourself now.

- On a sunny day, when the sky is clear, lie down on a lawn and make sure that when looking towards the sky there is nothing else in your field of view. Breathe deeply, observe every corner of the sky, every cloud that may pass by and every bird or animal you might see. Keep your ears open to perceive every little sound of the nature around you, be it the sound of wind, of a running river, of birds, other animals and so on. Pay attention to all the sensations on your body while you are on this lawn and feel the wonder of this moment that you are in complete contact with nature.

- At night, give yourself a few minutes to look up in the sky and silently observe the myriad of stars, planets and all the creation you can observe in the night sky. While you do this, bring your mind to understand how what you see is shrouded in an infinite immensity like the Universe. The sky you see is the same as all other human beings see and there is no difference. Expand this thought and see how the stars, the moon and all the other celestial objects are floating and are part of this big mystery that the Universe is. Perceive every new emotion or sensation that is created or appears to you while practicing the above. Also notice all the nocturnal sounds, of the wind, the trees, or animals around you.

Strong minds discuss about ideas, mediocre minds about happenings and weak minds about other people.

– Socrates

Key #6

Sensory Exercise

K ey #6 is a sensory exercise and it is the simplest and most powerful practice that enables us to get in deep contact with the present, the Now, and hence with our unconscious mind.

It is also one of the "secrets", we may say, of meditation, because having a total and complete sensory experience allows us to relax our mind, rather than stressing it even more, trying not to pay attention to external sounds or distractions.

The more sensory information we can perceive, the more the meditation (or self-hypnosis) will be deeper and beneficial for our mind and for our whole body and spirit.

Sensory Exercise

- Sit comfortably in a room that you like and feel safe in, possibly with many objects around and if possible, also open the window or sit where you can hear sounds coming from outside.

- Breathe deeply (inhale and exhale) for about 3 (three) times as you close your eyes and relax, placing your attention completely on your breath.

- When you feel you are relaxed enough, you can open your eyes and start seeing and noticing the things around you, the sounds you can hear, and the sensations you feel of your body.

- And now it is time to proceed with the exercise:

- Now, list and tell yourself 5 (five) things you can see, and say to yourself with your inner voice how and of what they are made of; what color, which material and get in as more details as possible.

- Now, list 4 (four) sounds you can hear and notice how they are made and describe details such as: intensity, volume, tone. Could be noises, voices, but also it could be the sound of your own breathing pattern, or even your heartbeat.

- Now, list 3 (three) sensations you feel on your body, such as your feet in your shoes and so on.

- Now, list 2 (two) scents you can smell and notice every detail and aroma.

- Finally, list 1 (one) flavor you feel in your mouth, now.

After completing this exercise, you can start again, from the beginning and you will see and notice how many new things and details you can perceive around you.

The more you repeat this exercise the more you will be able to live in the present and at the same time increase your capacity of sensory perception and awareness of the world around you and of the messages of your Unconscious Mind.

With continuous practice you will soon be able to see the results in more areas of your life by noticing the little everyday details in both your personal and work life.

Life will bring you pain all by itself.
Your responsibility is to create joy.

- Milton H. Erickson

Key # 7

Breathing Exercise

E ven if you have followed the 7 Key practices in the order presented in this book or even if you have not done so, you would probably have understood by now how the breathing patterns are fundamental keys to access that state of relaxation necessary or needed, and to be able to access your Unconscious Mind with ease.

You can find plenty of breathing exercises and all of them are equally great for you to try and explore, for your own benefit of your psycho-physical wellbeing.

Below you will find a straightforward and super effective breathing exercise whether you have performed or not a similar one before, or whether you are an experienced meditator or not. This is Key #7.

Breathing Exercise

- To fulfill this exercise in the most pleasant and functional way possible, I suggest you lie down on a lawn, or on your bed or on a very comfortable sofa. In addition, temperature is essential in this exercise and I suggest you cover yourself with a blanket, or a towel, or something that can keep you warm in case of a sudden change in the temperature of the environment in which you are practicing this exercise.

- Choose a nice background music and if possible, without any lyrics (I suggest frequency 432HZ) so that your exercise is accompanied by natural and pleasing sounds. The reason why I advise you not to listen to any other type of music is because the moment you relax and open your unconscious, you are much more influenced by external factors (such as advertising or other subliminal messages) therefore I prefer to advise you to the most suitable music for a pleasant and functional practice.

- Now, close your eyes and relax the muscles of your face, of your eyelids, of all the muscles around your eyes, your eyebrows, every little muscle in your head, your cheeks, relax the muscles of your mouth, every muscle until you reach the neck and as a result relax all your body down to your feet.

- Start breathing deeper than normal, now, and start directing all your attention to your breathing. Feel the air entering your nostrils, descend into your body and filling up your lungs. And as you exhale too, start feeling the air coming out of your lungs and your body and as you are doing that, now, you are relaxing, more and more each time.

- After about 5 (five) times that you will repeat this exercise you can begin to explore further this practice: Every time after you inhale, hold your breath until it is pleasant enough and then exhale and let go. Repeat this practice throughout the rest of the exercise.

- Now that you are getting the whole process, it is time to introduce more elements. Every time you inhale imagine the air you are breathing in, in a magnificent and shiny color, (the color you like the most) and imagine this color spreading and cover your whole body, while you hold your breath, until it is pleasant enough, bringing even more relaxation and even more beautiful sensations in every single cell of your body.

- And in the same way, every time you exhale, imagine that a dark and heavy air is leaving your body, now, and together with this air you are exhaling; you are also letting go of everything that is negative in your life, of everything you do not want or need in your life and of everything that is not good or necessary for you. So, now, exhale and let all those things, thoughts and feelings go out of your body, out of your mind and soul, so they can get lost in the vast infinite space...

- Every time you inhale, along with that shining and vibrant color of air that enters and fills your body, imagine seeing and feeling entering your body everything you want or need and everything that is necessary in your life, right now, all the emotions you need and want in your life, all the people you want to meet and all that is good for you, for your mind and soul.

- Continue this practice until it turns out to be easy and enjoyable, and every time your mind drifts away into wandering, keep your eyes closed, take a deep breath and return to put your attention on your breathing, relax and enjoy this moment of peace and gratitude.

I want you to get excited about who you are, what you are, what you have and what can still be for you. I want to inspire you to see that you can go far beyond where you are right now.

– Virginia Satir

Insight

The Unconscious Mind

*I*n this short insight I am pleased to present to you, in a simple manner, why it is so important to get to know your unconscious mind and why it is so important that you do explore it as deep as possible.

If there is an unconscious it is obvious that there is also a conscious and it is important to understand the difference and the relationship between these two parts of our mind.

The conscious mind is that rational, logical and critical part that makes us lose ourselves in self talk and leads us to create in our mind present or future situations that do not even exist and therefore create emotional states that stresses us and makes us experience symptoms such as anxiety.

The conscious mind is also that part that allows us to focus precisely on what we want to achieve and that allows us to create and plan effective and pragmatic goals and action plans.

It may seem complex to understand exactly how there can be another mind apart from this that I just explained above, and now I'll give you a practical example so that it is easier, for you, to understand what I mean.

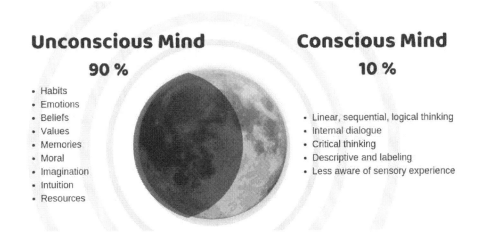

Unconscious Mind

90 %

- Habits
- Emotions
- Beliefs
- Values
- Memories
- Moral
- Imagination
- Intuition
- Resources

Conscious Mind

10 %

- Linear, sequential, logical thinking
- Internal dialogue
- Critical thinking
- Descriptive and labeling
- Less aware of sensory experience

Right now, while you are reading this book, you are looking at the letters flowing and you are paying attention to the meaning, and at the same time you are probably thinking, talking to yourself or even criticizing what you are reading or thinking; and that is your conscious mind at work right there.

At the same time while you are doing all the above you are also breathing; your eyelids are moving, and your heart is pulsating.

This is your Unconscious Mind working for you. In fact, this part of the mind takes care of your body and all its functions, besides being the dominion of all the emotions, the place where all the memories are recorded, cataloged and stored and sometimes suppressed if they contain a negative or painful emotional load still to be resolved.

If you want to solve traumas and negative memories of the past, so that you will be able to live freely without negative emotional loads such as stress or anxiety, and if you have that burning desire to get in touch even deeper with your Unconscious Mind. Get in touch with me.

The realm of the Unconscious Mind is 90% of our mind and it is also connected with all our neurology, be it the nervous system and all the muscles connected. Now you can better understand why sometimes when we feel stressed, we also start to feel pain in some parts of our body if we are oppressed by negative emotional loads or recurring thoughts that makes us feel unwell.

The Unconscious Mind has also all the answers we seek. It is the place where all the truth that we need in our lives is hidden, and that is, perhaps, why many times we do not want to pay attention to its voice, sensations, or signs.

Sometimes you prefer to live in a "comfortable" problem instead of having to face an inconvenient truth that certainly stretches and leads you to grow and improve as an individual and as a being in whole.

Knowing how to calm your mind, listening to your inner self, an Oracle of Delphi within our most sacred Temple, ourselves, is the most effective way to access your Unconscious Mind and your inner voice that can answer your every question.

This is the importance of knowing how to meditate, of knowing how to live in the present, in the now, and knowing how to have dominion over one's mind so that we can be in the here and now, be able to listen, rediscover our resources, live better and face the future without being misled by fictitious thoughts that leads us to weaken our body and our mind.

∞ ∞ ∞

"You are your only key to your success story, in your life, and it all starts in your Unconscious Mind.

– Thanos Kyng

Conclusion

On his throne, the King, was contemplating of all the memories, images, sounds, emotions that were in his mind. The Mage was still there, in front of him, enveloped in silence, waiting for the King to answer his questions.

It was so strange... since until few minutes ago the King had so many questions, and now, suddenly with the questions of the Mage, it is as if the clouds were gone from his mind and left room for the new, bright, rising sun...

The Mage, after the realization of the King during this mystical and loud silence, greeted with a nod and began step by step his way towards the exit of the throne room.

The King, in his confusion, stood up from his throne and still could not find the words to thank the Mage, so he raised one hand as if to greet that mystical figure, but the Mage had already left the throne room.

The Mage has the ability to listen and to ask the right questions to explore even more what the nature of these questions is. Granting a space for exploration and discovery where you, yourself, are both the explorer and the discoverer.

The King, at this very moment, understands that all the questions that have long been safeguarded and stored away in his unconscious mind are the keys to be able to discover The Truth that is within him...

Some of the keys are curiosity, research, and willingness to ask questions and to look for answers to your questions...

ΓΝΩΘΙ ΣΑΥΤΟΝ – Know Thyself, it is said In the Hellenic World.

Good Exploration of Your Unconscious Mind.

Extra Resources

Website:

www.thanoskyng.com

∞ ∞ ∞

Facebook Page with live streams, interviews, insights, events, and live seminars:

www.facebook.com/thanoskyngofficial/

∞ ∞ ∞

"EXPLORE YOUR UNCONSCIOUS MIND: 7 practices to find balance, serenity and energy for your everyday life"

by Thanos Kyng

Published by Mind Training International LTD

© 2019 London

Thanos Kyng
Visit my website www.thanoskyng.com

Isbn: 9781077455481

Printed in Great Britain
by Amazon